CW01261609

Original title:
Reflections of Possibility

Copyright © 2025 Swan Charm
All rights reserved.

Author: Kene Elistrand
ISBN HARDBACK: 978-9908-1-4873-1
ISBN PAPERBACK: 978-9908-1-4874-8
ISBN EBOOK: 978-9908-1-4875-5

Layers of Surreal Dreams

In shadows deep, where silence sighs,
Whispers of colors dance and rise,
Between the folds of night and day,
A canvas wakes, in hues of gray.

Lost in the labyrinth of thought,
What is imagined cannot be caught,
Floating softly on a stream,
Awakened souls in a lucid dream.

Veils of time, they drift and blend,
Reality bends where visions send,
Each breath a stroke, each heartbeat rhymes,
In the gallery of surreal times.

Fragments glimmer, pieces glow,
A paradox in ebb and flow,
In ethereal realms, we arrange,
The layers of dreams, strange and strange.

As dawn unfurls its gentle light,
The dreams recede, take flight from night,
Yet in our hearts, they softly gleam,
The echoes of our surreal dream.

Fractal Patterns in Time

In whispers of infinity, we find,
The echoing thoughts of a fractal mind,
Each twist a path, yet all entwine,
Endless beauty in the design.

Moments spiral, each one a part,
The pulse of existence, a rhythmic art,
Within the chaos, a structure shines,
Fractal patterns in cosmic lines.

Time cycles through its looping grace,
In every heartbeat, a sacred space,
Patterns unfold in the cosmic play,
Revealing truths in a dance of sway.

Dimensions echo, never align,
Yet in their discord, we define,
Paths that intersect, then unwind,
A tapestry woven, time's grand design.

As we traverse this endless maze,
In fractal wonders, we lose and gaze,
Each step reveals a hidden rhyme,
In the dance of fractals and time.

Tapestries of Becoming

Threads of essence, softly spun,
In every heart, a journey begun,
Woven colors merge and blend,
Tapestries of becoming, without end.

Each stitch a story, each knot a tale,
In the loom of life, we set our sail,
Winds of change caress our skin,
As we embrace the life within.

In moments fleeting, we craft and weave,
A fabric rich, which we believe,
Transforming sorrows into grace,
In the dance of time, we find our place.

Patterns emerge from chaos bright,
Illuminating paths in the night,
From threads that bind us, we arise,
Tapestries glowing 'neath starlit skies.

As life unfolds in vibrant hues,
We stitch together both bliss and blues,
For in the act of becoming free,
We find the threads that connect you and me.

Notes from the Edge of Tomorrow

Whispers echo from futures unseen,
In shadows of time, what might have been,
Notes in the wind, they flutter and sway,
From the edge of tomorrow, they find their way.

Faint melodies on the cusp of dawn,
As hopes weave dreams that linger on,
Moments suspended, waiting to soar,
Voices of promise, forever implore.

Through the veil of uncertainty's grasp,
Each heartbeat echoes, a fleeting clasp,
In the twilight glow, reflections play,
Notes from the edge, where thoughts stray.

Threads of fate intertwine and bend,
In luminous pathways, we seek to mend,
With every note, we shape and define,
A symphony born from the heart of time.

As tomorrow whispers secrets so near,
We gather the notes, dispelling fear,
In the dance of the known and unknown,
We write our future, together alone.

Realms Yet to Strike Dawn

In shadows deep where whispers fade,
Dreams awaken, unafraid.
The night holds secrets, ancient, vast,
While stars align, the die is cast.

A glimmer shines on distant hills,
With every breath, the silence thrills.
The nightingale begins to sing,
A promise held in early spring.

Through misty paths where spirits roam,
Each step we take leads us back home.
A world unfolds beyond the dark,
In dawn's embrace, a vibrant spark.

With every hue, the sky ignites,
Awakening dreams for new delights.
The horizon breaks, a canvas bright,
Where echoes of hope first take flight.

In realms yet known, our hearts will soar,
Boundless horizons forevermore.
Each dawn brings tales of life anew,
In every heartbeat, the world feels true.

Twilight of New Horizons

The sun dips low, a golden crown,
In twilight's glow, we wander down.
A whispered breeze through rustling leaves,
As day concedes, our heart believes.

Colors merge in a soft embrace,
As shadows dance, we find our place.
The world awakens, strange and bright,
In twilight's arms, we claim the night.

The mountains stand, a silent guide,
While rivers sing, their flow, our ride.
As stars appear in velvet skies,
Each twinkle tells of sweet goodbyes.

Hand in hand, we trace the line,
Where dreams converge, and souls entwine.
The night unfolds its tender charms,
Enveloped in each other's arms.

With every beat, a promise made,
In twilight's glow, our fears will fade.
New horizons wait beyond the light,
With hope and love, we chase the night.

Strokes of Creative Freedom

Brush and canvas dance together,
Colors blend like whispered dreams.
In the chaos, a spark ignites,
Art flows free, or so it seems.

Thoughts like rivers twist and turn,
Each stroke a story, bold and bright.
In the silence, passions churn,
Creating worlds in day and night.

Inspiration blooms in every heart,
Boundless as the endless sky.
From chaos, beauty finds its part,
In the freedom, spirits fly.

Bridges Over the Abyss

Stranded souls on either side,
Gaze across a chasm wide.
Hope builds bridges, stone by stone,
Unites the lost, the weary, alone.

Ties of laughter, threads of tears,
Span the void of doubts and fears.
With each step, courage swells,
Bravery in voices, love compels.

Together, hearts can find a way,
To cross the dark, to greet the day.
Hand in hand, we'll light the flame,
Bridges built, we'll be the same.

Lanterns Lighting the Path

In the dark, a glowing light,
Lanterns sway in gentle night.
Each flicker tells a tale of grace,
Guiding hearts to find their place.

Wisps of hope in shadows cast,
Illuminating dreams amassed.
With each step on this journey's road,
A brighter future, gently bestowed.

As we walk, together we'll see,
The way ahead, a tapestry.
Hand in hand, we move as one,
Lanterns guide until we're done.

Petals Unfurled with Hope

In the garden, petals bloom wide,
Softly brushing against the tide.
Each color whispers tales anew,
Of resilience, and love so true.

Raindrops kiss the fragile leaves,
Nature's promise, the heart believes.
In the sunlight, dreams take flight,
Petals soft in morning light.

Every bud, a story's start,
Ties together heart to heart.
With every breeze, let hope unfold,
In the petals, futures told.

Echoes of Tomorrow

In the dawn of a silent sky,
Dreams awaken, softly fly,
Carried by a gentle breeze,
Whispers of hope among the trees.

Each step forward, shadows fade,
Promises linger, never swayed,
Time dances on fleeting light,
Chasing shadows into night.

Voices linger in the air,
Songs of futures yet to share,
In the heart, the echoes ring,
Of all the joy tomorrow brings.

Paths entwined, a tapestry,
Woven with threads of destiny,
Every heartbeat, every sigh,
Carving stories in the sky.

So we journey, hand in hand,
Through the dreams we dare to stand,
Together, we shall find our way,
In the echoes of tomorrow's day.

Whispers of What Could Be

In the quiet of the night,
Stars twinkle with soft light,
Every dream a fleeting glance,
Whispers beckon, call to chance.

What lies beyond the known embrace?
A world anew, a stirring place,
With every thought that drifts and sways,
The heart ignites, begins to blaze.

Boundless visions in the mind,
Infinite paths, intertwined,
Each breath a choice to set it free,
To find the whispers of what could be.

Fleeting moments, dreams take flight,
Unraveling in soft moonlight,
When courage finds its place to grow,
The seeds of wonder start to flow.

So listen close, let your heart soar,
For within whispers lies much more,
In every pulse of what feels real,
The magic of life's hidden seal.

The Spectrum of Dreams Unfolding

Colors weave a vibrant tale,
Through the dusk and morning pale,
Every shade a whispered wish,
Filling hearts like a sweet dish.

Rainbows dance in the night's embrace,
Fleeting moments that we chase,
In every heartbeat, colors blend,
A spectrum that knows no end.

Each dream a brushstroke on the canvas,
Infinite visions, endless grandeur,
Transforming light in every way,
A kaleidoscope of night and day.

With every moment, hues expand,
Creating worlds just as we planned,
In the depths of night, they sing,
The joys and sorrows life can bring.

So let your spirit paint the sky,
And never fear to reach up high,
For in these dreams, we find our place,
In the spectrum, life's sweet grace.

Mirrored Horizons

Reflections dance on water's face,
Horizons meet in a warm embrace,
Every wave a story told,
In whispers bold, mysteries unfold.

The sun dips low, a golden hue,
Painting dreams in shades of blue,
With every dawn, a chance to see,
The mirrored horizons, wild and free.

Footprints left upon the shore,
Mapping wishes we explore,
As tides collide and worlds align,
In each moment, our souls entwine.

Glimmers of what lies ahead,
In every journey, words unsaid,
Through reflections in the sea,
We find the strength of how we'll be.

So look beyond, do not despair,
For in reflections, we find air,
In mirrored horizons, dreams collide,
Together, with the ocean, we glide.

Weaving the Threads of Dreams

In twilight's soft embrace, we find
Threads of silver, soft and bright.
Together they entwine and bind,
Creating visions in the night.

Whispers of hope dance on the breeze,
Intertwined with wishes pure.
Every thread brings heart's unease,
Yet dreams unfold; they shall endure.

Through shadows cast by doubt and fear,
We navigate with hands of grace.
Each stitch we take, so crystal clear,
Leads us to a vibrant place.

With colors drawn from the unseen,
We weave our tales, both bold and shy.
In the fabric of what has been,
Lies the promise of skies awry.

As dawn breaks forth, our dreams take flight,
Boundless realms of thought inspire.
In each new day, we chase the light,
Threads of dreams ignite our fire.

Chains of Emerging Realities

In the forges of our minds, we create,
Chains of thoughts, links intertwined.
Emerging paths we often debate,
Through choices made, our fates aligned.

Each link a moment, bright or dim,
Crafted from hopes, desires, and fears.
As life unfolds, we dance on a whim,
Through laughter shared and silent tears.

Reality shifts beneath our feet,
A tapestry of what could be.
In cycles of life, we feel the heat,
Transforming chains into a key.

Links of the past guide our next move,
Foundations built on what we know.
Yet in the chaos, we must find groove,
To embrace change and let it flow.

Together we rise, these chains we break,
Forging futures in rhythms free.
With every choice, the dawn we wake,
Emerging into our true decree.

Navigating the Unknown

In the mist where shadows fall,
We wander paths yet to be tread.
With hearts as compasses, we call,
Embracing all that lies ahead.

The stars above, our silent guide,
Illuminate the darkened sea.
With courage strong, we trust the tide,
Navigating what's meant to be.

Through valleys deep and mountains high,
We carve our hopes into the air.
Though doubts may rise and moments fly,
Our dreams persist, a soothing prayer.

In the unknown, we find our strength,
Each step a story waiting to bloom.
Together we travel, hand in length,
Turning whispers into a room.

As dawn approaches, light will flow,
Unveiling paths once hid from view.
With every breath, we gently grow,
Navigating skies forever new.

Dialogues with Destiny

In quiet corners, fate will speak,
Whispers dancing on the edge.
We gather strength, both bold and meek,
In dialogues that seamlessly pledge.

With every choice, a thread is spun,
Woven paths of chance and will.
Conversations begun, never done,
Each moment a chance to fulfill.

The universe listens, softly waits,
For echoes of our heart's desire.
In the space where wonder elates,
Destiny stirs, setting hearts afire.

With every heartbeat, a path unfurls,
Stories bloom with every word.
From stardust dreams, our fate swirls,
Through realms where heart and mind concurred.

So we converse with what shall be,
In this dance of time and chance.
With open hearts, we learn to see,
The beauty found in destiny's dance.

Seeds of Future Dreams

In the soil of quiet hopes,
Tiny seeds begin to grow.
With whispers of tomorrow's light,
They dance where breezes blow.

Nurtured by the spark of care,
In shadows of the tall old trees.
They stretch towards the shining sky,
Embracing all the gentle bees.

Each drop of rain a cherished gift,
Each ray of sun an open hand.
Together they will build a world,
Where dreams and daylight softly stand.

Roots dig deep in whispered tales,
Where every story finds its way.
With patience, love will cultivate,
The brighter paths of every day.

And when at last the flowers bloom,
A tapestry of vibrant hues.
We'll gather 'round this garden vast,
To celebrate our cherished views.

A Mosaic of Untaken Steps

Along the paths we dared not tread,
A mosaic waits to be defined.
Each piece a whisper of the past,
In fragments, memories intertwined.

The roads we did not seek to walk,
Are painted deep in shades of chance.
In every choice a story lives,
In every silence, a lost dance.

The footprints fade but never erase,
The laughter echoes in the air.
In shadows lie potential dreams,
That linger long, beyond compare.

Each untaken step, a lesson learned,
A chapter closed but not in vain.
For from the paths we choose to roam,
New journeys rise, from every pain.

So let us brave the undisclosed,
With open hearts and spirits free.
In every choice, a world awaits,
A limitless mosaic to see.

Light Through the Cracks

In weathered walls of muted gray,
The sunlight streams in golden beams.
Through cracks that time has gently worn,
Hope dances softly, weaving dreams.

Each ray a whisper from above,
A promise woven deep in time.
Illuminating all the dark,
With elegance in every climb.

Beyond the shadows, echoes play,
In corners where the silence stays.
The warmth creeps in, it draws us near,
To break the void of endless days.

And as we breathe in fiery hues,
Let every crack a story tell.
For through the wounds of broken hearts,
New light can shine, and all be well.

We'll cherish all the cracks in walls,
For through them, beauty finds a way.
In fractured moments, life reveals,
The light that guides us through the gray.

Pathways in the Mist

A veil of fog shrouds the morning,
As pathways twist and wander on.
With every step, the world unfolds,
In mystery before the dawn.

Where silence drapes the forest floor,
And whispers float on gentle breeze.
The unknown calls, a sweet allure,
To brave the trails among the trees.

Each footfall soft, a secret shared,
In nature's arms, we roam and find.
The paths that curl like ribbons bright,
Are trails of dreams intertwined.

In misty hues, the world transforms,
Each shadow dances, flickers light.
Through veils of gray, our spirits soar,
To seek the day, embrace the night.

So let us wander, hand in hand,
Through fog and light, in life's embrace.
For every step, though shrouded now,
Opens doors to hidden grace.

Shimmering Facets of Intent

In the quiet of the night,
Dreams dance like fireflies,
Whispers of unspoken wishes,
Painting stars across the skies.

Each thought a vivid jewel,
Sparkling with hope's embrace,
Guiding hearts through shadowed paths,
With light in every place.

Intent like golden sunrays,
Pierces through the misty veil,
Revealing truths long hidden,
Where souls refuse to bail.

A tapestry of visions,
Woven with threads of grace,
Each moment a reflection,
In this timeless, sacred space.

With shimmering facets bright,
We walk the path of dreams,
Embracing what lies ahead,
Together, or so it seems.

The Gateway to Unwritten Chapters

Beyond the threshold of today,
Opens a door to realms untold,
Where stories wait in quiet calm,
And destinies yearn to unfold.

Pages blank, yet filled with hope,
Ink of life yet to be penned,
Each heartbeat a gentle pulse,
Marking the starting blend.

With every step into the light,
Fear fades like morning mist,
Adventure beckons softly now,
In every twist and twist.

A call to write our legacy,
Ink of dreams, a vibrant flow,
With courage, we embrace the path,
To learn, to grow, to know.

So here we stand at dawn's embrace,
A canvas vast, a lively dance,
In the gateway to our future,
We leap bold, we take our chance.

Illuminated Steps into the Unknown

Beneath the canopy of stars,
We tread with hearts aglow,
Every step a whispered prayer,
Into the depths below.

With lanterns made of courage,
Guiding each uncertain pace,
We embrace the darkened paths,
With hope's warm, shining face.

The unknown calls with sweet allure,
A siren song of fate,
Inviting us to wander far,
And peer beyond the gate.

As shadows dance and twirl,
We find our rhythm's song,
In every twist of fate we take,
We know that we belong.

Illumined by our inner light,
We rise above our fears,
And with each step into the dark,
We find joy through the years.

A Symphony of New Beginnings

When dawn unfolds its golden wings,
A symphony begins anew,
Each note, a promise softly sung,
Inviting dreams to break through.

The orchestra of life's heartbeats,
Composes melodies divine,
With every rise, a fall in love,
Each moment we intertwine.

With every breath a fresh design,
Harmonies await our call,
New beginnings dance in the air,
In this grand, enchanted hall.

Fleeting moments, forever twined,
In rhythms of joy and pain,
Together we will write our score,
And sing through sun and rain.

So let us turn the page at last,
Embrace what lies ahead,
With hearts as full as symphonies,
We celebrate the threads we've shed.

Vibrations of Emergent Truths

In whispers soft, the truths arise,
Beneath the moon and starlit skies.
A pulse of light connects the hearts,
Awakening hope as darkness parts.

With every breath, new visions bloom,
In shadows deep, dispelling gloom.
The courage found in silent screams,
Ignites the fire of fractured dreams.

Across the void, we feel the sway,
Of ancient wisdom, come what may.
From every corner, voices blend,
In unity, we find our mend.

Like flowing rivers, thoughts entwine,
A sacred dance, divine design.
Each echo carries tales untold,
As souls unite, both brave and bold.

The song of life, a gentle hum,
In harmony, we all become.
Unraveled truths, they weave and twist,
In every moment, love insists.

Secrets within Unclosed Doors

A creak of wood, a whispered chance,
Holds hidden realms in silent dance.
With every step, new paths reveal,
The secrets that the heart can feel.

Peering through frames of time and space,
A glimpse of dreams we dare to trace.
The shadows speak, the light disturbs,
With every choice, the unknown curbs.

Unfolding wings of fears once pinned,
In every loss, new hopes rescind.
Unclosed doors breathe stories sigh,
Inviting souls to seek and fly.

With trembling hands, we turn the locks,
Untangling truths like nature's rocks.
Each threshold crossed, a world awaits,
Where mystery and wonder mates.

The heart, a compass bold and true,
Leads us where we can start anew.
In every journey, rich and poor,
Lie secrets still in unclosed doors.

Vaults of Inspiration

Within the mind, a treasure trove,
Where thoughts ignite and visions rove.
The vaults of dreams, so deeply stored,
Await our touch, their light restored.

In quiet moments, sparks ignite,
A canvas blank, a burst of light.
From whispered words and painted hues,
Creation stirs, enchanting muse.

A heartbeat quickens, passion flares,
In each pursuit, the spirit dares.
Unseen currents guide our hand,
Creating worlds we'll understand.

Through trials faced and losses borne,
In every crack, new hopes are sworn.
The depths we plumb, the heights we reach,
Inspiration flows, a sacred speech.

So take a chance, embrace the quest,
For every challenge brings us blessed.
In vaults of life, let visions blend,
Where every journey finds its end.

Peaks of Aspiration

Upon the heights, our dreams take flight,
In reverie of pure delight.
With every step, the view expands,
The summit calls with open hands.

Each peak we climb, a tale unfolds,
Of courage found in hearts of gold.
Our footprints mark the paths we tread,
As hopes arise where fears are shed.

The whispers of the winds declare,
The magic spark that's always there.
In twilight's glow, ambition sings,
As joy alights on fleeting wings.

Together forged by trials faced,
We seek the stars, our dreams embraced.
For every heart that dares to strive,
The peaks of aspiration thrive.

So lift your eyes, behold the call,
For in our unity, we stand tall.
With every summit, spirits rise,
Together reaching for the skies.

Threads of Unseen Futures

In the fabric of time, we weave,
Stories untold, dreams to conceive.
With threads of hope, we shape our fate,
Unraveling wonders, never too late.

In whispers of wind, futures call,
Strands of light, they rise and fall.
Choices like colors blend and swirl,
An endless dance in this vast world.

Each moment a stitch, a tale to spin,
Weaving paths where journeys begin.
Through shadows of doubt, we find our way,
Crafting a dawn from the end of day.

With every heartbeat, a new design,
Embarking on trails, shadows entwine.
In the loom of existence, we find,
Threads of resilience, ever aligned.

So let us create with skill and grace,
Embracing the unknown, we embrace.
For in these threads, our futures reside,
Waiting to bloom, like the rising tide.

Dancing with Potential

In the silence of dreams, we sway,
Steps of courage light the way.
With every twirl, possibilities rise,
In the glow of tomorrow, we improvise.

Whispers of daring lift us high,
As we leap into the boundless sky.
With fearless hearts, we chase the light,
Dancing through darkness, shunning fright.

Potential blooms in every glance,
A symphony of life, a vibrant dance.
We play our part on this grand stage,
Turning the page, we break the cage.

With laughter and hope, our spirits soar,
Unlocking the magic, forevermore.
The rhythm of dreams, our guiding beat,
As we pirouette on paths so sweet.

In the ballet of life, we find our role,
Every step written in spirit and soul.
Together we whirl in the cosmic flow,
Dancing with potential, forever to grow.

Shadows of Choice

In the corners of mind, shadows creep,
Choices like whispers, promises to keep.
Paths diverge in the twilight's hue,
What lies ahead, we cannot construe.

Every option, a delicate thread,
Tangled emotions, unspoken dread.
Yet in the silence, strength ignites,
As we embrace the unseen sights.

With each decision, a ripple unfolds,
Stories untold, brave and bold.
In the heart's chambers, echoes resound,
Navigating places yet unbound.

Through the maze of doubt, we bravely tread,
Facing the shadows, where fears are fed.
With courage we flicker, hearts in flight,
Choosing our fate in the fading light.

In the dance of decision, we find our way,
Transforming shadows into brighter day.
With every step that we dare to make,
We sculpt our destinies, no chance to break.

The Canvas of Yet

On the canvas of yet, our dreams unfold,
Strokes of imagination, stories untold.
Colors of hope blend rich and bright,
Painting the future with pure delight.

Each brushstroke whispers of what might be,
Possibilities woven, wild and free.
In the layers of now, we find our quest,
With every creation, we strive for the best.

As we scatter colors across the page,
The essence of life, we dare to engage.
In hues of laughter, in shades of tears,
We capture the moments that transcend years.

With hearts wide open, we craft and mold,
A tapestry rich, vibrant and bold.
For in every stroke, a piece of our soul,
Emerging as art, making us whole.

So let us paint with passion and zest,
On the canvas of yet, we are truly blessed.
For the masterpiece waiting, none can forget,
Is the promise of tomorrow in the art of yet.

Threads of Unwritten Tales

In shadows deep, where dreams reside,
Whispers weave, our hearts collide.
Each thread a wish, a story spun,
Beneath the stars, we've just begun.

Page by page, the ink will flow,
Winding paths where secrets grow.
The tales we tell, both fierce and bright,
Illuminate the darkest night.

In every twist, a lesson learned,
With every flame, our passion burned.
The loom of life, it stretches wide,
Connecting souls, with hope as guide.

So gather close, and share your dreams,
In every heart, a spark redeems.
Let's weave our fates with threads so bold,
In unwritten tales, forever told.

For in this dance, we find our grace,
A tapestry of time and space.
With every stitch, a bond we make,
Our stories shared, for love's own sake.

Winds of Change

The winds they blow, with whispers sweet,
They shake the leaves, and stir our feet.
A gust of hope, a chill of doubt,
In every breath, we're called to shout.

From mountain high to valley low,
The winds will guide where we must go.
With every turn, a choice unfolds,
A tale of courage, yet untold.

As clouds drift past, new skies appear,
With winds of change, we must not fear.
They carry dreams on currents strong,
Adjustments made, we'll find our song.

In stormy nights, and sunny days,
These shifting winds, they urge our ways.
To break the chains that hold us fast,
Embrace the change, the die is cast.

So let the winds dance through your soul,
Awaken passion, make you whole.
For in each gust, a chance to grow,
A brighter path, the winds bestow.

Fragments of Wonder

In shards of light, the world does gleam,
Each fragment holds a hidden dream.
In tiny moments, magic brews,
A whispered thought, a secret muse.

Through morning dew and evening tide,
The wonders bloom, cannot hide.
In nature's hand, a fragile grace,
In every heart, a sacred space.

With eyes wide open, we explore,
The beauty in the unseen lore.
In every glance, a story waits,
In scattered pieces, love creates.

So gather these fragments, hold them near,
For in their depths, there lies no fear.
Embrace the chaos, find delight,
In every spark, let hope ignite.

In humble things, the wonder flows,
Unraveled dreams, like rivers, flow.
With every breath, we learn to see,
The magic lies in you and me.

Streams of Ambition

In quiet streams, our hopes arise,
Flows of ambition, reaching skies.
Each drop a dream, a vision bright,
Together we chase the morning light.

The currents push, they bend, and sway,
They carve our paths, come what may.
In raging winds, or gentle ease,
With heart and mind, we'll find our keys.

Let boundaries fade, like mist at dawn,
With every heartbeat, we move on.
Through twists and turns, we pave the way,
In streams of ambition, we shall stay.

The mountain high, the valley low,
In every struggle, seeds we sow.
With passion's fire, and courage's call,
We'll rise together, never fall.

So wade on through, the water's fine,
In every ripple, dreams align.
With steadfast hearts, let visions ring,
In streams of ambition, we take wing.

Seeds of Imagination Sprout

In garden beds where dreams take flight,
Tiny seeds of thought ignite.
With gentle hands, we sow the ground,
In fertile minds, ideas abound.

With sunlight's touch and raindrops grace,
Imagination finds its place.
Roots of wonder start to grow,
A vibrant world begins to show.

From whispers soft to shouts of cheer,
Each vision nurtured, crystal clear.
In every heart, a spark can bloom,
Transforming silence into room.

Together we shall tend this land,
With hope and trust, we take a stand.
Emerging dreams, our shared delight,
As seeds of imagination take flight.

Beyond the Known Skyline

Beyond the hills, the sun will rise,
A canvas painted in the skies.
With colors bold, and shades unheard,
Adventure waits, our spirits stirred.

The horizon calls, a siren's song,
It pulls us forth, where we belong.
With every step, new paths unfold,
A story written, brave and bold.

The stars above guide our way,
In dreams we trust, come what may.
Through valleys deep and mountains high,
We'll chase the dawn till day runs dry.

So hand in hand, we'll face the light,
With hearts aflame, we'll soar in flight.
In every heartbeat, every sigh,
We journey forth, beyond the sky.

Cascading Echoes of Hope

In the valley where shadows dwell,
A whisper rises, soft and swell.
Each note a promise, bright and clear,
A symphony of hope we hear.

Through darkest nights, it weaves its way,
A silver light to guide the stray.
With every chime, it breaks the chains,
Resilience born from joy and pains.

The echoes travel, far and wide,
They speak of love that won't divide.
In every soul, a spark ignites,
Cascading dreams, reaching new heights.

So let the music of the heart,
Be where our healing journeys start.
With harmonies that never cease,
We'll find our way, in perfect peace.

A Tapestry of Infinite Pathways

Threads of fate entwined with care,
In every choice, a pathway there.
Colors blend, a vibrant weave,
In this mosaic, we believe.

With every step, new patterns form,
In life's grand dance, a quiet storm.
We twist and turn, embrace the chance,
In every heartbeat, a sacred dance.

The winding roads may lead us far,
Yet in our hearts, we hold a star.
A lighthouse guiding through the night,
Illuminating love and light.

So let us journey, hand in hand,
Through valleys deep and golden sand.
Together weaving, strong and free,
A tapestry of you and me.

Shimmering Dawn of Promise

The sun peeks over hills of gold,
Illuminating dreams yet untold.
A gentle breeze whispers through the trees,
Awakening hearts, bringing ease.

With every ray, a new chance blooms,
Chasing away the shadowed glooms.
The world is painted in vibrant hues,
As hope rekindles and love renews.

Clouds drift apart in the morning light,
Creating paths that feel so right.
Each moment dances with pure delight,
As day replaces the folds of night.

In this dawn, we rise hand in hand,
Embracing the beauty of this land.
Together we stride, hearts all aglow,
In the shimmering dawn, we choose to grow.

As promises whisper on the breeze,
We find strength in the rustling leaves.
This day unfolds, a canvas so vast,
The shimmering dawn sets our spirits free.

Portraits of the Possible

Brush strokes etch dreams on the canvas bright,
Imagining futures, filled with light.
Each color a story, a vision to see,
Reflecting the essence of who we can be.

In the gallery of hopes, we dare to explore,
Each portrait a window, revealing much more.
Moments captured, emotions so deep,
In frames filled with promise, our spirits leap.

The artist's touch brings shadows to dance,
Reviving aspirations, giving them a chance.
With every glance, inspiration ignites,
As visions of tomorrow take beautiful flights.

Through diverse lenses, we gather in peace,
Crafting a world where all thrive and increase.
Together we stand, in unity's glow,
Creating a gallery of hope we bestow.

With colors of kindness, we paint the day,
In portraits of possible, we find our way.
Embracing the beauty of every small part,
These artworks of life, a celebration of heart.

Shades of Harmonious Hopes

In fields of green where dreams intertwine,
Shades of hope blossom, brightly they shine.
Beneath a sky painted with stars so bright,
We walk in harmony, hearts full of light.

A symphony plays on the gentle breeze,
Melodies whisper through rustling trees.
Each hope a note in hearts that believe,
Creating a world where we dare to achieve.

The colors of laughter mix with our tears,
Blending together, dispelling our fears.
In every shade, courage finds foothold,
As we paint our futures in stories retold.

From whispers of dawn to dusk's sweet sigh,
The spectrum of life stretches far and wide.
In unity's embrace, our spirits unite,
In shades of harmonious hopes, we take flight.

So let's dance in the hues of what's to come,
Together, we'll sing our vibrant anthem.
With arms wide open, we welcome the dawn,
In this kaleidoscope, our spirits are drawn.

Cascades of Courage

Rushing water flows, fierce and free,
In cascades of courage, we find the key.
Each drop a tale of strength untold,
Carving paths vibrant and bold.

Through rocky terrain, the river fights,
Braving the darkness, embracing the lights.
Every splash tells of battles won,
Waves of resolve under the sun.

In moments of stillness, we gather our might,
Reflecting on struggles that brought us to light.
The power within us flows like the stream,
Cascades of courage, we rise and we dream.

Together we navigate life's shifting course,
Finding strength in unity, a binding force.
The waters may churn, but we stand our ground,
In cascades of courage, our souls are found.

So let the currents take us where they may,
With hearts full of bravery, we'll seize the day.
In the rhythm of life, we'll flourish and thrive,
Cascades of courage keep our dreams alive.

Cadence of Adventure

In the whisper of the breeze, we roam,
Paths unknown, we call them home.
Stars above, our guiding light,
Every step feels vibrant, bright.

Mountains rise, we climb so high,
Chasing dreams beneath the sky.
Rivers flow, wild and free,
Nature sings our melody.

Footprints left on sandy shores,
Echoes of our hearts' great roars.
With each dawn, new tales unfold,
Embracing life, brave and bold.

Winds of change, they softly blow,
Through the valleys, valleys low.
With courage held in every hand,
We create, we understand.

Adventures weave, a tapestry,
Coloring our history.
Through meadows lush, through shadows deep,
The adventure lives, our spirits leap.

Shards of Light in Dark Places

In the shadows, hope ignites,
Flickers soft in darkest nights.
Every tear a lesson learned,
From the ashes, fire burned.

Voices murmur, whispers sweet,
Through the pain, we rise to meet.
Stars emerge from clouds so gray,
Guiding us along the way.

Fragments of a shattered heart,
Healing slowly, piece by part.
Grateful for the scars we wear,
With each mark, a story shared.

In the silence, strength we find,
Courage whispered, intertwined.
Light will come to those who seek,
Shards of brightness, brave and meek.

Together we find solace near,
In the dark, we cast out fear.
With hope's glimmer, together we rise,
Shards of light in endless skies.

Labyrinths of the Heart

In the chambers of the soul,
Winding paths, we seek to whole.
Every turn, a choice we make,
In this dance, our hearts awake.

Secrets whispered, shadows cast,
Lessons learned from ties that last.
With each heartbeat, echoes sound,
Finding love, where lost is found.

Twists and turns, the thrill of fate,
Timing's dance, we contemplate.
In the maze, we sometimes stray,
Yet the heart will find its way.

Colors blend, emotions flow,
Through the highs and deepest low.
Guided by the stars above,
In this labyrinth, we find love.

Through the chaos, we emerge,
Unified, our spirits surge.
In the heart's own maze, we thrive,
Together, we truly arrive.

Tides of Hope and Fear

Waves crash high upon the shore,
Pulling dreams forevermore.
With each tide, a lesson learned,
Hope and fear, fate's wheel turns.

Beneath the moon, the waters gleam,
Dancing shadows, chasing dreams.
In the depths, uncertainty waits,
Yet courage never hesitates.

As the sun sets, colors blend,
In our hearts, the will to mend.
With every rise, the shadows fade,
Brighter days, unafraid.

Oceans vast and wide as night,
In their depths, we seek the light.
Through the surges, we will steer,
Navigating hope and fear.

Hand in hand, we face the tide,
Together, none have to hide.
With love's anchor, we shall gain,
Through the storms, we will remain.

Resonance of Aspirations

In silent dreams, we take our flight,
Aiming high, like stars at night.
Voices echo, hopes unwound,
In every heart, ambitions found.

With every step, a whisper calls,
Promises dance in shadowed halls.
United souls in fervent chase,
In the light, we find our place.

Through valleys low and mountains steep,
We guard the visions that we keep.
A symphony of voices rise,
Together, we shall touch the skies.

Each challenge met, we stand as one,
Forging paths beneath the sun.
In passion's fire, we ignite,
The dreams that bloom in darkest night.

So let us soar on wings of grace,
For each ambition finds its space.
Resonance of what can be,
In every heart, a wild decree.

Tides of New Beginnings

The dawn breaks soft, a canvas bare,
Each wave whispers, a call to dare.
From shadows deep, we rise anew,
With courage bold, to see it through.

A gentle tide, it pulls us near,
Washing away the weight of fear.
In every ripple, a chance to grow,
As the wind of change begins to blow.

With open hearts, we embrace the ride,
In shifts of fate, we take our stride.
Each moment holds a spark of light,
Guiding us towards what feels right.

The horizon calls, a beacon bright,
Leading us through the dark of night.
In every glance, a future found,
With open arms, we stand our ground.

So let the tides wash fears away,
For every end brings forth a day.
In the dance of life, we find our song,
Tides of new beginnings carry us along.

Murmurs of Tomorrow's Canvas

On the edge of dreams, we stand awake,
Painting futures, choices we make.
In whispers soft, the colors blend,
Murmurs hinting at paths that wend.

Brush strokes light upon the page,
Crafting visions filled with sage.
Each moment captured, ever bright,
In the heart, they take their flight.

From shadows cast, we sketch the dawn,
With every heartbeat, we respond.
The palette rich, with hopes to share,
A masterpiece beyond compare.

In gentle tones, aspirations hum,
To rhythms of change, we all succumb.
With every sigh, a wish takes shape,
Murmurs of dreams in colors drape.

So let us draw with passion's hand,
Creating beauty, spark a brand.
Tomorrow's canvas waits in grace,
For every heart to find its place.

Chasing Fleeting Visions

In the twilight, shadows weave,
Fleeting whispers we believe.
Chasing dreams like butterflies,
With open hearts and hopeful eyes.

They dance and flutter, just out of reach,
Lessons learned, the heart's own preach.
With every heartbeat, we pursue,
Visions bright and skies so blue.

In every turn, a chance to seek,
The courage found in moments weak.
Through sunlit days and starry nights,
We chase these visions, ignite new lights.

Each breath we take, a move toward fate,
In timeless rhythms, we navigate.
With every step, we break the seal,
The magic found in how we feel.

So hold the visions close, so dear,
For every dream brings us near.
Chasing shadows, light will show,
The beauty of the paths we grow.

Fluid Paths of Becoming

Like rivers twist and turn,
We find our way through life.
Each bend reveals new dreams,
In flow, we shed our strife.

Shadows dance in fleeting light,
Moments swirl like whispers.
With every drop that fades,
A new path starts to shimmer.

Trust the currents strong and true,
Embrace the ebbs and flows.
Transformation waits ahead,
In fluid grace, it grows.

We rise from quiet depths,
Emerging into air.
Each struggle molds our form,
Crafting beauty, unaware.

As seasons shift and change,
We learn to let things go.
Fluid paths of becoming,
Lead onward, heart aglow.

Glimmers of What Lies Ahead

In the twilight of the dawn,
Hope begins to light the way.
Glimmers spark our weary hearts,
Turning night into day.

With dreams like fragile stars,
We reach for what we seek.
Each moment, filled with promise,
In silence, visions speak.

The horizon calls us forth,
With colors bright and rare.
Glimmers of what lies ahead,
Whisper dreams in the air.

Though shadows may surround,
We carry light within.
Guided by the faintest glow,
New journeys can begin.

Together, we ignite,
The fire in our souls.
Glimmers shining brightly,
Illuminate our goals.

Uncharted Journeys Within

In silence, we discover,
The paths we've yet to tread.
Uncharted journeys within,
We venture without dread.

Each heartbeat a compass,
In depths of the unknown.
Lost whispers lead us onward,
Embracing what we've grown.

Like echoes of the past,
We forge new histories.
In every twist and turn,
We rewrite our own keys.

Explore the hidden spaces,
Where fears and dreams collide.
Uncharted journeys within,
Bring strength we can't divide.

Together we will wander,
Through forests of our minds.
In these uncharted lands,
A newfound peace we find.

The Turning Point of Existence

At the edge of what we know,
A flicker stirs within.
The turning point of existence,
Where life begins to spin.

With courage, we embrace change,
As shadows start to fade.
Each heartbeat marks a moment,
In choices we have made.

Time shifts like endless tides,
As dreams reweave their thread.
The turning point of existence,
Where new paths lay ahead.

In the dance of life's embrace,
We find our true intent.
Every step, a revelation,
In wisdom's arms, we're lent.

Awake to every heartbeat,
In unity, we grow.
The turning point of existence,
Is where our spirits know.

Murky Waters of Opportunity

In the depths where shadows dwell,
Opportunities hide and swell.
With a whisper, they call my name,
In murky waters, I seek the flame.

Glimmers of hope through the haze,
Navigating through the maze.
Courage builds as fears recede,
From the depths, I plant the seed.

Echoes linger in the night,
Shaping dreams with silent might.
In murky depths, I chart my way,
For hidden gold in disarray.

Each current pulls, a gentle guide,
Through the unknown, I'll still abide.
With each stroke, the waters part,
Revealing pathways, a brand new start.

So embrace the swirling tide,
In murky waters, I'll reside.
For every chance holds a story,
In shadows, I find my glory.

Spheres of New Constructs

In circles wide, new worlds arise,
Constructs that challenge, mesmerize.
Each sphere a chance to redefine,
Creating dreams, a grand design.

Ideas dance like fireflies,
Illuminating darkest skies.
With visions clear, we shape the day,
In vibrant hues, we find our way.

Minds converging, hearts aligned,
In spheres we seek, our truths enshrined.
With every thought, a bridge we build,
Fostering change, our spirits thrilled.

Through layers thick, we dig and dive,
In new constructs, we come alive.
Each sphere a map to navigate,
As we converge to co-create.

In unity, we break the mold,
Transforming dreams into pure gold.
In these spheres, our hope ignites,
Constructing futures, scaling heights.

Lifting the Veil of Doubt

Beneath the shadows, doubt resides,
A heavy weight that oft divides.
With gentle hands, I lift the veil,
To find the truths that never fail.

Whispers of hope weave through the night,
Eclipsing fears with dawning light.
In every heartbeat, courage grows,
As I confront what doubt bestows.

Each step I take, a path revealed,
Breaking chains that once concealed.
Through open eyes, I dare to see,
The strength within, the chance to be.

With every breath, I rise anew,
Embracing what I thought I knew.
In lifting doubts, I find my voice,
In vulnerability, rejoice.

For from the veil, a spirit free,
Unbound by chains, at last, I see.
In lifting doubt, I find my way,
To brighter tomorrows, day by day.

Refractions of the Soul's Yearning

In prisms bright, emotions play,
Refractions whisper night and day.
The soul, it aches, it seeks to find,
A deeper truth, a love unconfined.

Through shattered glass, the colors gleam,
Each hue a fragment of a dream.
With every glance, a longing stirs,
The heart's soft beat, in silence purrs.

In search of warmth, the spirit roams,
Across vast lands, it calls me home.
Refractions dance in fleeting light,
Embracing shadows, clutching bright.

The yearning echoes, deep and wide,
Each moment lived, a sacred guide.
Through all the chaos, I will trace,
The soul's sweet cry, the tender embrace.

In every tear, a story gleams,
In every smile, a thousand dreams.
Through refractions, love appears,
The soul's longing, through all the years.

Eclipses of the Conventional

In shadows fall the shaped norms,
Reality bends, its essence warms.
A dance of thoughts, a daring chase,
We shatter the glass, rewrite the space.

With whispers soft, we question the day,
Old paths dissolve, new colors sway.
Through twilight's gaze, we find our light,
In mystery's grip, we rise in flight.

The stars collide, ideas take form,
Emerging truths, a vibrant storm.
In midnight's grasp, the air ignites,
Breaking the silence of sacred nights.

We paint the skies in hues profound,
With every breath, the lost is found.
An echo rings through realms of thought,
A revolution, courage sought.

When shadows merge, the new is born,
In chaos, beauty, a world reborn.
We embrace the void, let go of chains,
In the void's embrace, our spirit reigns.

Maps to the Unknown

Beneath the stars, uncharted lands,
We follow roads with trembling hands.
With every step, a tale unfolds,
In silence whispers, the brave and bold.

The compass spins, no pointed aim,
Adventure sings its timeless name.
We seek the paths not drawn in ink,
Where dreams ignite and doubts now shrink.

Through valleys deep and mountains high,
We chase the clouds along the sky.
In shadows cast, our courage glows,
The heart's desires gently grow.

Each twist and turn, a chance to learn,
With open hearts, we yearn and burn.
The map is blank, yet we feel its pull,
The essence of life, exploratory and full.

With every step, we write our tale,
Guided by stars, we cannot fail.
In the unknown, our spirits soar,
With hope as our anchor, we seek for more.

Radiant Designs of Fate

In threads of gold, our stories weave,
A tapestry rich, destined to believe.
With hands entwined, we craft the day,
In luminous paths, our dreams display.

A dance of colors, vibrant and bright,
In shadows deep, we find our light.
Each stroke a choice, each moment a grace,
In radiant designs, we find our place.

With every heartbeat, our fates entwined,
In cosmic flows, the truth we find.
Together we soar, together we fall,
In the fabric of time, we're part of it all.

With whispered wishes, the stars conspire,
To spark the flame of our deepest desire.
In intricate dreams, our hopes align,
In the dance of fate, we dare to shine.

Each moment a canvas, each breath an art,
In the light of our dreams, we play our part.
Through radiant designs, we navigate,
In every turn, we celebrate fate.

Starbursts of Imagination

In night's embrace, the visions spark,
A realm of wonders, shining dark.
With every thought, a star ignites,
Illuminating the quiet nights.

In swirling colors, dreams take flight,
Chasing shadows, crafting light.
With open minds, we sketch the skies,
In starbursts bright, our spirit flies.

Through galaxies vast, we dare to roam,
In the heart of wonder, we find our home.
The universe whispers, a cosmic tune,
Beneath the magic of the moon.

Each twinkle a spark, each flash a chance,
In the dance of stars, we take our stance.
With fearless hearts, we leap and dive,
In imagination's glow, we come alive.

From fantasies wild to wishes small,
In the tapestry of dreams, we weave them all.
In starbursts bright, we paint the night,
With every heartbeat, we take flight.

Echoes of Dreamscapes

In twilight's glow, dreams unfold,
Silhouettes dance, stories untold.
Whispers linger on the breeze,
Carving memories like ancient trees.

A soft embrace from stars above,
Cradling hearts in tales of love.
Each echo found in twilight's light,
Guides the soul through endless night.

Through shadowed paths, the dreamers stride,
Painting visions, side by side.
Reality seems but a fleeting game,
As echoes call, yet none can tame.

Reflections dance on silver streams,
Weaving through the fabric of dreams.
In depths of silence, secrets rest,
Holding the tangled threads of quest.

So take my hand in this wonder,
Where time stands still, and hearts grow fonder.
In echoes soft, let us reside,
As dreamscapes weave our souls like tide.

Veils of Tomorrow

Beneath the clouds, horizons gleam,
Unraveled threads of a whispered dream.
With every dawn, a promise swells,
In veils of tomorrow, hope compels.

Painted skies in shades of gold,
Awaiting tales that dare be told.
The future dances on the breeze,
In gentle motions, hearts find ease.

Time's embrace nurtures each wish,
A tapestry woven in life's rich dish.
Through every triumph, every tear,
Veils of tomorrow draw us near.

Uncertain paths may lie ahead,
But we find courage when love is fed.
With each heartbeat, new dreams rise,
Underveiling worlds beneath the skies.

Together we walk through dreams unknown,
Planting seeds, our truth is sown.
In veils of tomorrow, we'll find our way,
As hope ignites the coming day.

Glimmers of Unseen Paths

In shadowed corners, whispers call,
Glimmers of paths where shadows fall.
With each step, the heart beats strong,
Navigating this world so long.

Threads of light weave through the night,
Guiding souls towards the bright.
In silence, listen; dreams ignite,
As unseen paths come into sight.

Mysteries dance along the way,
Whispers of truth in daylight's sway.
With every turn, new wonders lie,
Inviting us as we learn to fly.

The journey unfolds in breaths unsaid,
Glimmers emerge from the fears we shed.
Among the stars, we find our muse,
As unseen paths become our views.

So take a step towards the light,
Embrace the glimmers in the night.
In wanderlust, we forge our fate,
For in these paths, we quiet fate.

Whispers of What Might Be

In quiet corners, dreams take flight,
Whispers linger in the night.
Possibilities dance in the air,
Tales of wonder, beyond compare.

With every breath, a new chance grows,
In the stillness, the heart knows.
What might be, lingers at dawn,
A tapestry of light to adorn.

Hope flutters like pages turned,
In the furnace of passion, embers burned.
Embrace the whispers, let them be,
Guiding souls to what might be.

Through shadow and light, we must roam,
In every heartbeat, we find our home.
Each whisper speaks of endless dreams,
Fueling life's vibrant schemes.

So gather the whispers, let them sing,
What might be flows on gentle wing.
In each moment, life finds a way,
Through whispers, we create the day.

Luminescence of Untold Journeys

In the hush of twilight dreams,
Footsteps whisper on the seams,
Stars awake with glimmer bright,
Guiding souls to endless flight.

Waves of time, they crash and flow,
Lifting hearts where shadows grow,
Paths diverge in moonlit gleams,
Charting maps of vivid dreams.

Voices call from distant lands,
Tracing lines with gentle hands,
Journey forth, the world ignites,
Luminescence in the nights.

Secrets held in breezes soft,
Roots entwined in ancient loft,
Every step a tale retold,
In the light, the brave unfold.

Endless tales in twilight's grasp,
From the past, to future clasp,
Rise with dawn, let spirits soar,
Untold journeys, forevermore.

Dances of the Unimagined

In the realm where shadows play,
Dreams and hopes begin to sway,
Rhythms pulse beneath the skin,
Unseen worlds await within.

Footsteps turn on unseen floors,
Whirling winds open new doors,
As the music shapes the night,
Dancing souls take joyful flight.

Colors splash in wild disarray,
Painting paths in bold ballet,
Every twirl, a secret spun,
Crescendo of the beating sun.

Hold your breath, let silence roam,
In the dance, we find our home,
Moments flicker, hearts ignite,
In the spark, purest delight.

Through the void, the rhythm calls,
Echoes weave within the walls,
Untamed leaps and joyous cries,
In unimagined skies.

Horizons of Infinite Choices

Beneath the vast cerulean dome,
Every glance, a path to roam,
Horizons stretch, a painter's dream,
Flowing lines, like a winding stream.

Mountains rise where hopes ascend,
Every bend can fate amend,
Choices whisper on the breeze,
Guiding hearts with gentle ease.

All decisions, small or grand,
Built on dreams, like castles stand,
Future's light can shift and sway,
Illuminate the brightest way.

In the twilight, visions blend,
Each horizon finds its end,
Step by step, the journey flows,
In the heart, the courage grows.

Infinite pathways await,
Open doors to create fate,
With each choice, a seed to plant,
In the garden of what we want.

Shadows of Potential

In the stillness of the night,
Whispers linger, dreams take flight,
Shadows dance upon the wall,
Echoes of the times we fall.

Beneath each veil, a secret lies,
Unseen wings that yearn to rise,
From the depths, a spark will glow,
Fires of hope begin to flow.

Every shadow, a silent tale,
Within the light, we will not fail,
Trust the paths that lay ahead,
In the dark, our dreams are fed.

Potential waits in every breath,
New beginnings born from death,
From the silence springs our strength,
In the shadows, we find length.

So embrace the night's embrace,
In its arms, find your own grace,
For from shadows, we emerge,
Into the light, our spirits surge.

Lighthouses of New Perspectives

In dusk's embrace, they stand so tall,
Guiding hearts through shadows' call.
With beams that pierce the foggy night,
They spark the spark of inner light.

Each wave that crashes on their shore,
Whispers secrets, tales of yore.
New paths emerge with every tide,
Inviting journeys deep inside.

They teach of hope amidst despair,
With every flicker, every flare.
Illuminating the darkest fears,
Transforming pain to shedding tears.

A dance of colors in the sky,
As storms of doubt pass swiftly by.
With steadfast warmth, they keep us true,
To paths where dreams are borne anew.

So let them shine, these beacons bright,
In guiding us toward the light.
For every choice that we can make,
Can lead to journeys, hearts awake.

Gardens of What Could Be

In whispered winds, dreams take their flight,
Soft petals gleam in morning light.
Each seed a hope, each branch a way,
To nurture visions day by day.

Among the blooms, the colors blend,
A tapestry that will not end.
The fragrance rich, a tempting tease,
Invites us near with gentle ease.

Paths winding through the lush expanse,
Where every turn invites a dance.
The soil holds stories, deep and wide,
Of all the journeys they provide.

Each flower's face, a bold embrace,
In quiet corners, find your place.
Through thorns and trials, strength revealed,
In gardens vast, our hearts are healed.

So let us plant with love and care,
The tendrils of our dreams laid bare.
With every bloom, a vision free,
In gardens vast of what could be.

Kaleidoscope of Choices

Within the glass, a world unfolds,
A dance of colors, tales retold.
Each turn reveals a different view,
A spectrum rich, of old and new.

With every shift, paths intertwine,
In patterns strange, our hearts align.
Fractals spinning, choices bright,
In vibrant hues of wrong and right.

The echoes whisper, options tease,
A fluttering heart seeks to appease.
From darkened corners, light can spring,
In every choice, a song to sing.

So let the colors guide your hand,
In realms of fate, where dreams expand.
The joy of living, found in chance,
A joyful, ever-changing dance.

In life's great art, be bold and free,
Embrace the shift, the mystery.
For every lens will show a way,
A kaleidoscope of bright array.

Echo Chambers of the Mind

In silence deep, reflections play,
The thoughts parade in light and gray.
Each echo bouncing off the walls,
A world contained in whispered calls.

Within the chambers, voices blend,
Ideas clash, and some offend.
Yet through the noise, a truth can rise,
If we can dare to change our ties.

A cavern vast, where fears reside,
With shadows lurking, hope can hide.
But listen close, to gentle tunes,
For wisdom shines beneath the moons.

With every thought, a choice we make,
To break the mold or ride the wake.
To challenge what we think we know,
And let fresh winds of change to blow.

So find the strength to shift the view,
In echo chambers, forge the new.
For within the mind, a world can thrive,
Where every thought can come alive.

Flickers in the Abyss

In shadows where secrets dwell,
Flickers of light weave and swell.
Whispers of dreams, barely seen,
Echo in silence, a hidden sheen.

Moments of truth, lost in time,
Shapes of the past in rhythm and rhyme.
Fleeting thoughts take flight and roam,
Searching for solace, a place called home.

Eyes that wander, souls that yearn,
In the abyss, the candles burn.
Flickers of hope, fragile yet bold,
Stories of love that never grow old.

The darkness stirs, a tender sigh,
Sad melodies drift, and then goodbye.
In the embrace of the night we cling,
To all the wonders the shadows bring.

Chasing the moments, lost in despair,
Yet the flickers persist, we find them rare.
Each gleam a promise, a daring wish,
A gentle caress, the heart's soft swish.

Corners of the Uncharted

In corners where silence breathes,
Wonders await, like whispered wreaths.
A map unfurls, drawn with dreams,
Leading to paths where adventure gleams.

Winding trails kissed by the sun,
Stories wait where the rivers run.
Each step forward, a mystery grows,
In the shadows, a soft wind blows.

Secrets shiver, ancient and grand,
Carved in the earth, marked by hand.
A tapestry woven, threads of gold,
In corners unseen, the brave behold.

Echoes of laughter, a distant cheer,
In the unknown, we shed our fear.
With hearts ablaze, we chart our quest,
In corners of dream, we find our rest.

Adventurous spirits, wanderers bold,
Embrace the stories yet to be told.
In the uncharted, horizons expand,
With each new venture, hand in hand.

Glances at the Infinite

A gaze that lingers, time standing still,
Moments unfold as the heart feels the thrill.
Stars ignite, piercing the dark,
Glimmers of truth in each tiny spark.

The universe whispers in soft, sweet tones,
Echoes of love in celestial groans.
With each glance, we touch the divine,
In realms of wonder, where secrets align.

Clouds drift past, carrying thoughts,
Moments of peace where the soul is caught.
In endless spaces, we find our way,
Glances at magic, night turns to day.

The infinite calls, a soft, gentle force,
Guiding us onward, revealing the source.
Life is a dance, a vivid embrace,
Glances at beauty in boundless space.

With every heartbeat, the cosmos sings,
Connecting us all, the joy it brings.
In the eternal, we lose, then find,
Glances at life, both gentle and blind.

Crescendos of Unfolding

In layers of sound, stories arise,
Crescendos breaking, like brightening skies.
A symphony swells, hearts intertwine,
Moments unfolding in sweet, pure design.

Notes that whisper, then crash like waves,
Carrying dreams through the heart's hidden caves.
With each crescendo, we rise and fall,
Echoes of life, the anthem calls.

Softly we gather, voices in tune,
Dancing with shadows beneath the moon.
As crescendos echo, we bravely unite,
In the symphony's warmth, we take flight.

Harmony blossoms, tender yet bold,
In the music of life, our stories unfold.
Each note a heartbeat, a breath, a chance,
Crescendos of joy in the grandest dance.

Together we weave in dimensions unknown,
Crescendos of love beautifully sown.
With each note played, the universe sings,
In the crescendo of life, our spirit takes wings.

Dive into the Enigma

Beneath the waves, the secrets hide,
A world unknown, where dreams collide.
In shadows deep, where whispers play,
Dive deeper still, let go, and sway.

Curious hearts seek paths unseen,
With every splash, a chance to glean.
Unravel knots of time and space,
In the depths, find your embrace.

A dance of thoughts, a swirling bliss,
In silence, hear the ocean's kiss.
Each ripple holds a tale profound,
In enigma's arms, we are unbound.

From tides that pull to currents strong,
In mystery's grip, we all belong.
Explore the dark, the unexplored,
In depths of awe, let spirit soared.

Rivers of Untold Stories

Flowing gently, whispers flow,
Carving paths where silence grows.
Every bend a tale unfolds,
In twilight's glow, each heart beholds.

Reflections dance on mirrored streams,
Carrying fragments of forgotten dreams.
From mountain high to ocean wide,
In rivers deep, our hopes abide.

Wanderers pause, listen in,
To currents swift, where tales begin.
With every drop, a life lived well,
In currents strong, their stories swell.

The quietude speaks, the water sighs,
In every wave, a truth defies.
Through woeful tears or joyous song,
In rivers deep, we all belong.

Sailing forth, we recognize,
The ties that bind beneath the skies.
In mingled flows, our spirits roam,
In rivers wide, we find our home.

Veins of Possibility

In the quiet pulse of night,
Lie paths untold, dreams take flight.
Branches stretch with hope aglow,
In every pulse, a way to grow.

With every heartbeat, choices hum,
Through shadows dark, new ventures come.
In whispers soft, the future calls,
Embrace the chance, let caution fall.

Veins of dreams entwine and weave,
In tapestry rich, we dare believe.
Each venture starts with just one step,
In realms of bright, the fear can wept.

Eyes wide open, horizons clear,
In every moment, magic near.
With courage bold, we navigate,
In veins of hope, we create fate.

In vibrant beats, together throng,
Through twists and turns, we all belong.
In life's embrace, possibility,
In every breath, we shape our sea.

Whirlpools of Transformation

In whirlwinds spun, change does bring,
A cycle fierce, transformation's sting.
In the heart of chaos, stillness grows,
With every spin, new life flows.

The eddies swirl, a dance profound,
In depths unseen, we are unbound.
Through torrents wild, we find our way,
In swirling tides, night births the day.

Embrace the churn, the fierce embrace,
For from the storm, we find our place.
In currents strong, our spirits soar,
The whirlpool calls, forevermore.

A spiral high, above the fray,
In radiant dawn, we greet the day.
Through every rise, through every fall,
In transformation's grip, we hear the call.

With change as guide, we journey forth,
In whirling paths, we find our worth.
In every turn, new dreams ignite,
In whirlpools deep, our souls take flight.

Collages of Infinite Possibilities

A canvas spread with hues untold,
Fragments of wishes, brave and bold.
Each piece a story, woven tight,
In the tapestry of day and night.

Whispers of colors dance like fire,
Dreams glimmering with pure desire.
The heart's mosaic ever grows,
Beneath the sky, where freedom flows.

Countless paths intertwine and blend,
A journey where no limits end.
With each heartbeat, new tales start,
Infinite visions from the heart.

Time's gentle hand shapes and molds,
Creating wonders yet untold.
In these collages, life's essence sings,
Infinite possibilities on fragile wings.

Here we gather, voices clear,
United in hope, casting fear.
Together we paint this grand design,
In every corner, our dreams align.

Castles in the Air

Whispers of laughter, visions soar,
Building dreams on heaven's floor.
Each brick a wish, each tower a chance,
In the clouds, our spirits dance.

Gilded spires reaching high,
Fingers trace the endless sky.
Moments crafted, light as air,
Imagination's realm, beyond compare.

Through the mist, our hopes ignite,
A realm where wrong feels right.
Every imagine, boldly explored,
Castles stand where dreams are stored.

Floating gently, we rise anew,
Each heartbeat, a vision true.
As shadows play on distant hills,
We nurture hopes, the heart fulfills.

In the silence, dreams unite,
Beneath the stars, we chase the light.
With open hearts, we dare to share,
In the beauty of our castles in the air.

Silhouettes of Uncharted Dreams

In twilight's grasp, we find our place,
Silhouettes drift with elegant grace.
Veiled in mystery, futures gleam,
Each shadow whispers an unseen dream.

Twisted paths of night unfold,
Secrets hidden, stories told.
With every step, we press ahead,
Guided by stars, where angels tread.

On the canvas of the darkened night,
We paint our hopes with gentle light.
Flickering moments, fragile and true,
In every heartbeat, our dreams renew.

A tapestry stitched with starlit threads,
Mapping the journeys where passion spreads.
Together strong, we sail the stream,
In the silence, we build our dream.

With open arms, we greet the dawn,
Silhouettes fading, yet never gone.
For in the waking, our hearts take flight,
Uncharted dreams burst into light.

Portals to Altered Realities

Through silver gateways, worlds align,
A dance of spaces, hearts entwine.
In whispered echoes, secrets play,
Portals open to a brand new day.

Step inside, the veils will shift,
Magic drapes our souls a gift.
In every breath, a shift in time,
Dreams ripple softly, like a rhyme.

Reality bends and sways anew,
Currents of time, an ocean blue.
Each portal holds a tale immense,
Fragments of life weave through suspense.

With each heartbeat, we dive deeper,
To realms where visions become keepers.
Our spirits soar, breaking the mold,
In altered states, we find the bold.

Together we wander, hand in hand,
To places where possibilities expand.
In this unknown, we find our light,
Portals beckon, dreams take flight.

Embers of Change

In twilight's glow, the embers gleam,
Whispers of hope in the fading beam.
Flickers dance in the night's embrace,
A world reborn, a fleeting trace.

With every sigh, the winds will shift,
Carrying dreams, a radiant gift.
From ashes rise, new paths unfold,
In the heart of night, brave souls bold.

Through shadows deep, the light will spark,
Guiding lost hearts in the dark.
Change is wild, yet beautifully near,
In the warmth of hope, we hold dear.

Emerge and grow, like blossoms rare,
Fresh beginnings, in healing air.
Embers glow where doubt once stood,
Transforming pain into something good.

The Alchemy of Aspirations

In the cauldron of dreams, we stir the fate,
Mixing our desires, we contemplate.
Gold from the mundane, visions align,
In the magic of moments, we dare define.

With courage as our steadfast flame,
We forge our paths, refusing blame.
Essence of will, we plunge so deep,
In the heart of night, our promises keep.

From ashes rise, the phoenix's flight,
Transforming pain into pure delight.
Alchemy whispers in the still night air,
Building our future with tender care.

Each wish a note in a cosmic song,
We dance through the chaos, resolute and strong.
A tapestry woven of hope and gold,
In the alchemy of now, our dreams unfold.

Celestial Maps of What Lies Ahead

Star-stitched skies guide our way,
Charting a course, come what may.
In constellations, stories weave,
Each twinkle a promise, a chance to cleave.

Through nebulae of dreams unspoken,
Boundless paths where chains are broken.
Galaxies whisper, their wisdom old,
In the interplay of shadows bold.

Celestial maps, drawn with care,
Guide our hearts through the cosmic air.
With every heartbeat, we chart the sea,
Navigating by the pulse of destiny.

In planetary rhythms, we find our flow,
As stardust empowers the seeds we sow.
The universe hums a melodic grace,
In the dance of time and endless space.

Grains of Time in the Hourglass

Each grain a moment, slipping fast,
Echoes of laughter, shadows cast.
In the hourglass, time's gentle dance,
A fleeting glimpse of every chance.

With open hands, we catch the now,
Embracing the present, making a vow.
To savor the sweet, the bitter too,
In the tapestry spun, we find the true.

As sands cascade, our lives unfold,
In every story, a memory told.
Within the glass, both joy and pain,
Moments cherished, the lessons gained.

Though time may flee with a soft caress,
In every heartbeat, we find our rest.
Grains of time in the hourglass,
Whisper of life, in memories, we amass.

www.ingramcontent.com/pod-product-compliance
Ingram Content Group UK Ltd.
Pitfield, Milton Keynes, MK11 3LW, UK
UKHW051540281224
452712UK00025B/597